BMX
STREET

Patrick G. Cain

Lerner Publications Company • Minneapolis

Lerner Publications Company
A division of Lerner Publishing Group, Inc.
241 First Avenue North
Minneapolis, MN 55401 U.S.A.

Website address: www.lernerbooks.com

Content Consultant: Cody York, professional BMX photographer

Library of Congress Cataloging-in-Publication Data

Cain, Patrick G
    BMX street / by Patrick G. Cain
      p. cm. — (Extreme summer sports zone)
    Includes index.
    ISBN 978–1–4677–0751–0 (lib. bdg. : alk. paper)
    1. Bicycle motocross—Juvenile literature. I. Title.
  GV1049.3.C347 2013
  796.6'22—dc23   2012020762

Manufactured in the United States of America
1 – PP – 12/31/12

Photo credits: The images in this book are used with the permission of: Backgrounds: © Cody York/ www.codyyorkphotography.com, 4-5, 6, 7, 8-9, 12, 14, 20, 20-21, 23, 24, 25, 26, 28, 28-29, 29 (top), 29 (bottom); © Mary Evans/Universal Pictures/Amblin Entertainment/Ronald Grant/Everett Collection, 8; © Reed Saxon/AP Images, 10; © Harry How/Getty Images, 11; © George Olsson/ iStockphoto, 13; © Ben Haslam/Haslam Photography/Shutterstock Images, 15; © Bernard Girardin/ Fotolia, 16; © Catherine Lane/iStockphoto, 17; © Jorg Hackemann/Shutterstock Images, 18; © Peter Kim/Fotolia, 19; © Brett Beyer/Getty Images, 27

Front cover: © Michael Sharkey/Stone/Getty Images (main); © RTimages/Shutterstock.com (background).

Main body text set in Folio Std Light 11/17.
Typeface provided by Adobe Systems.

TABLE OF CONTENTS

CHAPTER ONE

WHAT IS BMX STREET RIDING?

In the late 1980s, BMX rider Craig Grasso was a king among kings. He was a BMX vert rider. Vert riders use giant ramps called half pipes. They race up the ramps and catch air (make a jump) to do tricks. However, Grasso paved the way for a new style of BMX: street riding.

In 1987 Grasso had a famous run that captured the pure rebellion of BMX riding. At the 2HIP King of Vert competition in California, Grasso did a run completely naked. It was a sign of BMX street riding's future. Street riders still have similar rebellious attitudes when they invent tricks and ride.

SAFETY FIRST

In professional street events, many riders don't wear pads or helmets. But when they practice, they usually wear safety gear. By the time most BMX street riders compete, they have perfected every move. But mistakes still happen. In 2011 pro rider Van Homan fractured his skull during the X Games. After his injury, many events began requiring helmets. Accidents are dangerous. They can also cost a rider his or her career. If a pro can't ride because of an injury, that rider may lose sponsors and not make money.

Van Homan is one of the best BMX street riders around. But even he takes hard falls sometimes.

Street riding is one of the newest types of BMX riding. It didn't become widely known until the 1990s. Street riding is similar to vert riding, but street riders don't use half pipes or jumps. Instead, street riders do smaller tricks that can be performed off everyday objects.

BMX street riders take ordinary objects and find new ways to use them. Every curb, handrail, or picnic table is a chance for a new trick. The sport takes incredible amounts of balance, strength, control, and practice. Pros make BMX street tricks look easy, but tricks take a lot of practice. And practicing new moves often means taking hard falls. That is why riders should take whatever safety precautions they can. Being safe is incredibly important in BMX street riding.

BMX riders make videos of themselves riding so they can share their talent with the world.

Thanks to events such as ESPN's X Games, BMX street riding has become very popular. Modern BMX street riding professionals are highly paid stars. And street riders don't have to participate in the X Games to become famous. Daring riders film themselves all over the world. Then they share their videos online and let the world judge them. What was once a sport centered in Southern California is now a lifestyle shared around the globe.

THE X GAMES

Since 1995 ESPN has held an extreme sports competition called the X Games. This is the biggest competition in extreme action sports such as BMX. Like the Olympic Games, X Games winners compete for gold, silver, or bronze medals. Winners also earn prize money. The X Games is the showcase for many never-before-seen tricks. Pro riders will often work for months, trying to perfect their routines or specific moves.

CHAPTER TWO

BMX STREET'S BEGINNINGS

A s far back as the 1960s, motorbikes revved up and raced around dirt tracks in California. But not everyone who wanted to ride the track could afford a motorcycle. Kids started taking their road bikes on these dirt courses. These kids started a revolution. The new sport was known as bicycle motocross. The name was eventually shortened to BMX. Soon kids were taking their bikes off the dirt courses and into empty swimming pools and skate parks.

By the early 1980s, the sport had made it big. BMX bikes began making appearances off the track. Steven Spielberg's 1982 movie *E.T.: The Extra Terrestrial* even included a getaway scene on BMX bikes.

E.T. was one of the first popular movies to feature BMX bikes.

The BMX bike was here to stay. By 1983 freestyle BMX events were becoming more common. These events featured riders doing stunts rather than racing.

One rider, Bob Haro, created a special bike frame just for freestyle BMX riding. The frame was designed to be strong and tough. It was also able to handle the steep ramps BMX riders were beginning to use for vert riding. The modern BMX bike was born.

In 1984 Ron Wilkerson successfully completed the first no-footed aerial. During his jump, he took his feet off the pedals. Riders began experimenting with more extreme tricks. They put tricks together to make combinations, which riders call combos.

MAT HOFFMAN

Mat Hoffman's success as a rider has helped him launch his brands Hoffman Bikes and Hoffman Promotions. These brands teamed up with ESPN to help create the X Games. Hoffman has created more than 100 tricks. He is the only person to execute a no-handed 900 (he sped up a ramp and spun around in the air two and a half times while on his bike) during a competition. With his talent for tricks and business skills, Hoffman has helped make BMX street what it is today.

The Birth of Street Riding

The first street contests were held by the 2HIP Society, a BMX group Wilkerson founded. Street riders were still not as well known as other types of BMX riders. However, the street-riding movement was growing. In 1989 famous BMXers Mat Hoffman and Eddie Roman released the 31-minute-long video, *Aggroman*. The short film featured BMX riders doing some of the first street-riding tricks.

Mat Hoffman helped make BMX biking what it is today.

Rider Brad Simms competes in the BMX street elimination round during the 2010 X Games.

It showed sequences of tricks by Hoffman, Roman, and other top riders. The movie was rough and low quality. But it showed BMX street riding at its best.

In 1991 Hoffman changed the BMX world once again. He started a bike company called Hoffman Bikes. The company designed bikes that were built for street tricks. Hoffman also hosted the Bicycle Stunt Series, a series of competitions dedicated to BMX riding. He included street riding as an event. The Bicycle Stunt Series was a big hit.

In 1995 ESPN held its first Extreme Games competition, shortened to X Games. BMX's popularity continued to rise. BMX bikes at this time were starting to look more like modern BMX bikes. Riders were taking off their brakes, riding with pegs, and pulling off even more incredible moves.

BMX riding also began appearing on national television and in popular video games. Pro riders and businessmen Dave Mirra and Hoffman both created popular video games for the PlayStation. Skateboarding legend Tony Hawk endorsed a video game that also

OBSTACLES

Street-riding courses are designed to be similar to the streets the riders practice on. Street courses include many objects, known as obstacles. Riders use these obstacles to create tricks. Each course is different. Some examples of obstacles are quarter pipes, park benches, ledges, handrails, or even cars. The obstacles themselves also vary by course. Ledges may be different heights, from flat to 4 feet (1.2 meters). Handrails might be round or square. Some handrails even have kinks (drops in the handrail). These elements add to the challenge of tricks. Whatever the street course obstacles are, they copy what riding in the streets is really like.

featured BMX riding. Hawk's game became one of the most popular extreme sports video games.

Riders still did flashy tricks in vert events. But street riding's popularity was picking up. The tricks street riders created on quarter pipes, a smaller type of ramp, began appearing in events. Without big ramps, street riders had less opportunity for big air. That meant riders had to be even more skilled to land these moves during street competitions.

BMX street riders, like Dakota Roche, use quarter pipe ramps to create tricks.

CHAPTER THREE

THE BRANDS, EQUIPMENT, AND MOVES

P roper equipment is part of the game. BMX gear and the street style that comes with the gear make up the BMX street lifestyle. BMX riding is famous for brands that create this street style, such as Vans, DC, FOX, Cult, and Animal Bikes. For a rising BMX star, becoming sponsored by one of these big-name companies is a big deal.

The Brands of Street Riding

Every sport has certain brands people associate with it. For BMX riding, brands are enormously important. If it weren't for the support of sponsoring brands, BMX street

Rider Bobby Simmons is sponsored by Vans and several other brands. Getting sponsored is a big deal for BMX riders.

Mountain Dew sponsors
the Dew Tour, which
features several BMX
events.

riding may have never taken off. The athletes who helped make BMX street riding a mainstream sport relied on the sponsorships from these brands to make money. Becoming a professional rider is a full-time job and requires lots of practice. Without the brands, pro riders likely couldn't support themselves financially and still have enough time to ride.

Companies such as ESPN, Red Bull, and Mountain Dew sponsor BMX competitions. They bring the daring riders and their incredible tricks to an audience. Before these competitions, riders relied on magazines for exposure. BMX fans could only read about the exciting tricks their heroes were pulling off. Now BMX fans can watch their favorite stars showing off on live television.

The Equipment

You can't play baseball without a bat and a ball. And riders need special BMX bike pieces if they want to compete in street events. But the bikes haven't always had these special parts. Modern BMX bikes look very different from the bikes that first made BMX riding popular. New BMX bikes can be built from a variety of different materials. Chromoly steel is best for street BMX bikes. The bikes take a lot of rough falls and high-stress tricks that a softer metal such as aluminum can't always handle. BMX bike frames come in sizes ranging from micro to pro XXL. The rider's height decides what size is best for a rider.

BMX bikes need to be tough to handle the tricks riders put their bikes through.

Some riders choose to buy their bike already assembled. Other riders build their own bikes piece by piece. Whether their bikes are preassembled or custom-built, riders often want to upgrade parts or change their bikes' style. BMX bikes keep getting better. As riders continue pushing the limits of their tricks, they find new ways to improve their bikes. There's no end to the new stunts that riders can invent.

THE SCHWINN STING-RAY

The leading tool of the BMX revolution was a bike called the Schwinn Sting-Ray. The Sting-Ray was the Ferrari of bicycles. Riders felt unbeatable on its long seat. By 1968 about 70 percent of all bikes sold in the United States were Sting-Rays or copycat versions of the Schwinn classic. With the bike's good handling, kids were popping wheelies and riding dirt trails. These early riders were the inspiration for many of the riders who define what BMX street riding has become.

Schwinn Sting-Rays were the original BMX bikes.

Safety First!

Proper equipment for riders is more than just bike parts. BMX riders need to stay safe to keep riding. According to the pros, here are three must-haves:

Bike helmet: BMX riders use bowl helmets with a hard plastic outer material. With different colors and patterns, a rider's helmet can be just as expressive as a street routine the rider creates.

Knee pads: Even though BMX pedals have extra grip, a rider's feet will occasionally slip. If they do, the rider's knees could get knocked around. The pads also protect a rider's legs from other spills while practicing a new move.

BMX gloves: If a rider does fall, BMX gloves are good to have. Ripping up a palm on gravel is not any fun.

Stay safe when BMX biking by wearing a helmet and gloves. Many riders wear knee pads under their jeans.

A BMX rider pops a wheelie. Although not all riders wear helmets, it's a good idea to wear one. One bad fall can cause a serious injury.

The Moves

Bunny Hops and Wheelies

Bunny hops and wheelies are some of the easiest moves a rookie BMX rider can do. In a bunny hop, the rider jumps both the front and back wheels of the bike off the ground at the same time. In a wheelie, the rider lifts the front wheel off the ground, balancing on the back wheel.

Spins

A spin is another common trick for a BMX street rider. A beginning rider may try a 180. To do a 180, a rider jumps, spins, and lands facing the opposite direction from which the rider started. More advanced riders may try a 360 (one full spin) or a 540 (one and half spins), and more. A rider might then add other elements, such as removing his or her hands from the handlebars.

Garrett Reynolds pulls off a truckdriver at the 2010 X Games.

Bar Spins

To do a bar spin, a rider spins the handlebars all the way around. This will only work if the front wheel is off the ground. Riders often combine bar spins with other moves. With a lot of practice, a rider might be able to do a 360. Adding a bar spin to the 360 will make the stunt even more impressive. This move is known as a truckdriver.

Foot Plant

A foot plant is a great way for a rider to turn the bike around and perform a cool trick at the same time.

Turn a
Round
ahead

When getting close to a surface such as a wall or a quarter pipe, the rider plants a foot on it, pivots, and catches air. Then the rider lands while riding in the direction he or she came from.

Grinds

Grinds or peg grinds are another common trick for BMX riders. This is when a rider jumps the bike and lands on an object, such as a handrail. Then the rider slides across the object using the bike's pegs.

BMXer Chad Ring does a double peg grind.

CHAPTER FOUR

BECOMING A BMXCHAMPION

BMX street riders don't have a professional league like baseball or football players. They also don't have a regular season where fans can count on seeing them face off. That's one of the major reasons BMX freestyle events have not yet made it to the Olympic Games. However, BMX racing was introduced to the Olympic Games in 2008. So an Olympics BMX street competition may be in BMX riding's future.

Most street riders get together and simply ride with or without an audience. But when a major sponsor is able to get all the riders in an area together, the street heroes face off. At these competitions, riders compete as individuals. They are judged for creativity and technical skill. The runs are a test against themselves as much as a competition against others. Riders jump over and off boxes. They get big air on ramps. They grind on rails. Bikers create extreme runs as fans cheer them on.

Nina Buitrago does a toboggan move. Female riders may be able to compete in the X Games in the near future.

NINA BUITRAGO

Men dominate the BMX world. However, professional women ride too. Women's events are starting to appear in competitions across the world. Since the early 2000s, Nina Buitrago has been a leading freestyle BMX rider. When she started riding, many people who ran bike companies said women couldn't ride BMX. Just a few years later, those same companies were asking to sponsor her. Buitrago now rides for a few different companies. She has ridden for the massive show company Etnies since 2005.

Veteran BMXer Van Homan does a tailwhip at the 2009 X Games. Homan won the X Games street silver medal in 2008 and bronze in 2009.

What Are the Events?

Each year several major events bring together the top BMX street riders. Red Bull sponsors BMX street competitions throughout the year. The Summer X Games and Mountain Dew's Dew Tour take place every year. The Dew Tour also has an amateur series. Rookie riders who win in the amateur series have a shot at competing in the professional Dew Tour. Since 2008 Garrett Reynolds has been one of the best pro street riders. He won the X Games BMX street competition from 2008 to 2012 and is known for a lot of fast-paced, difficult moves. His runs show what the competitions are all about: pros having fun on their bikes and showing fans amazing tricks.

What's Winning?

In a street competition, riders are judged on the difficulty of their moves and the style of their trick routine. If a rider makes his or her tricks as long and smooth as possible, the rider may get a high score for style. At the ESPN X Games, the score is based on both difficulty and style. A perfect score is 100 points. No rider has ever received a perfect final score for BMX street.

GARRETT REYNOLDS

When Garrett Reynolds is on, he is unstoppable. His X Games winning streak started in 2008. Since then, his skills and intense speed powered him to four ESPN X Games gold medals in a row. He was the first rider to ever win five straight championships.

Garrett Reynolds won the gold medal in BMX street competition every year from 2008 to 2012.

Nina Buitrago (left) and Angie Marino (right) are working to spread the word about female BMX riding.

Where to Watch?

ESPN's X Games is shown on national cable television. But BMX street riding in the X Games only comes once a year. Fans who don't want to wait can have a parent or an adult help find videos online. Street highlights from pros and amateurs alike are available through video-sharing websites

ANGIE MARINO

Angie Marino is a pro rider who is sponsored by a Scottish bike company. She has competed in BMX contests around the world. She and Nina Buitrago are best friends. Fans often see them riding together. Marino works hard to promote female BMX riding. She has been trying to convince major BMX events, such as the X Games, to add more female classes to their competitions.

Becoming a great BMX street rider means lots of practice.

such as YouTube. (Beginning riders need to be careful, however. Trying to copy the moves shown online can be a quick way to get injured!)

Go to the Street

Professional and amateur riders practice all the time. Most BMX street riders will never get sponsored or make it to the X Games or a Dew Tour event. But they still love to ride and do tricks with their friends. BMX street riding is not about winning or losing. Street riders practice and ride because they love it.

THE BREAKDOWN OF A BMX BIKE

TOP TUBE

This is the top piece of a bike frame. Riders choose the length of their top tubes based on how tall they are.

GEARS

BMX bikes don't change gears the way other bikes do. One common setup is a big gear in the front that has 25 teeth connecting to a smaller gear on the back wheel that has nine teeth. The gears and wheels are connected in a style called freewheel. Freewheeling allows bikes to pedal backward without the bike braking or changing directions.

WHEELS

BMX bike wheels are much wider than wheels on other bikes. Most pros use wheels 20 inches (51 centimeters) wide or wider. A skinny wheel couldn't withstand all the force riders put on it when performing tricks such as jumps or bunny hops.

HANDLEBARS

BMX street bike handlebars also come in different sizes. Most BMX handlebars have rubber grips. A detangler rotor is connected to the handlebars. This allows a rider to spin the handlebars without tangling up the brake cables if a rider is using a bike with brakes.

PEDALS

BMX street riders prefer a pedal known as a platform pedal. A platform pedal is larger than those used on other types of bikes. It also has lots of grip so riders can make tough landings without their feet slipping off.

CRANKS

The pedals are connected to the gear using a three-piece tubular crank.

PEGS

Pegs allow riders to do more tricks, such as grinds. Most riders use bikes with four pegs: two in the front and two in the back.

GLOSSARY

AMATEUR
someone who participates in an activity for fun without expectation of payment

COMBOS
groups of tricks done together

FREESTYLE
a type of BMX biking where riders do tricks rather than race

HALF PIPE
a ramp used in extreme sports that looks like half the inside of a pipe

MAINSTREAM
something that is normal or commonly accepted

PROFESSIONAL
someone who participates in an activity as a job for payment

QUARTER PIPE
a ramp used in extreme sports that looks like one-quarter of the inside of a pipe

ROOKIE
someone who is new to a sport or activity

RUN
a set of tricks

SPONSOR
a company that financially supports an individual so they can focus on an activity

FOR MORE INFORMATION

Further Reading

Cain, Patrick G. *BMX Vert*. Minneapolis: Lerner Publications, 2013.

Dick, Scott. *BMX*. Chicago: Heinemann Library, 2003.

Savage, Jeff. *Dave Mirra*. Minneapolis: Lerner Publications, 2007.

Thomas, Isabel. *Freestyle BMX*. Minneapolis: Lerner Publications, 2012.

Websites

ESPN X Games
http://espn.go.com/action/xgames
The official X Games website features information about the X Games. Check out BMX athlete bios, videos, and scores, and find out when and where the next X Games will be held.

Kidzworld Action Sports
http://www.kidzworld.com/sports-zone/action-sports
This website includes information about BMX biking and other action sports.

Livestrong.com BMX
http://www.livestrong.com/bmx/
This website provides facts about BMX biking. It includes information on safety gear, BMX history, and more about the world of BMX biking.

INDEX

About the Author

Patrick Cain is a nuclear engineer turned writer. He is an award-winning journalist whose work often appears in a number of magazines such as *ESPN, The Magazine*, and *Fast Company*. He currently lives in Los Angeles, California, but will forever be tied to upstate New York.